Velvet and Barbed Wire

A collection of Poem

By Ankita Roy

pencil

ISBN 9789362638588

Published in India 2025 by Pencil

A brand of
One Point Six Technologies Pvt. Ltd.
Unit no. 26, Ground Floor, Building A1,
Wadala Truck Terminal Road,
Near Post Office, Antop Hill, Mumbai - 400037
E connect@thepencilapp.com
W www.thepencilapp.com

Author biography

Ankita Roy, is a first-time poet whose debut collection is only a glimpse into the world she has quietly built in the pages of her diaries. Though new to publishing, she has long been a keeper of words—writing in silence, not for an audience, but for the comfort of release and reflection.

Her poetry is born from raw emotion, fleeting thoughts, and the kind of feelings that often go unspoken. For years, her notebooks held the weight of her inner world—filled with verses no one knew existed. Now, with this second book after "Scribbles Beneath the Bed", she opens the door just enough to let others in.

Ankita writes not to impress, but to connect—with anyone who has ever felt too much and said too little. This collection is her second, but it carries the depth of someone who's been writing her whole life.

CONTENTS

Preface

This book was never meant to exist—not like this.

These poems were born in the quietest hours, written not for eyes, but for survival. They lived tucked between diary pages, in the margins of notebooks, in the silence between heartbeats. I never planned to share them. I never thought I could.
But feelings have a way of asking to be seen.

This collection is a map of what I couldn't say out loud—an attempt to put shape to the shapeless. You won't find perfect rhymes or clever metaphors in every line. What you'll find instead are pieces of me: the soft, the broken, the wondering, and the still healing.
If you've ever felt something too deeply to name… these pages are for you.

Let this be not a book of answers, but a quiet place to feel. A place where no one knows, yet somehow, everything makes sense.
— Ankita Roy

Acknowledgements

To my mother and father—

Thank you for being my first home, my first truth, and the quiet strength behind every word I've ever written. Your love, even in silence, has shaped me more than I can say. This book holds pieces of everything you've given me—kindness, resilience, and the courage to feel deeply.

To those who stood beside them—family, friends, and kind strangers—Whether you stayed or walked away, you left behind lessons I carry still. Some taught me how to hold on. Others, how to let go. All of you, in your own way, helped me become someone brave enough to write this.

This book is not just for those who stayed, but for those who passed through and left something behind—grace, ache, memory, or meaning.
Thank you for the footprints. I followed them here.
— Ankita Roy

1. She Let Go of the Desk

This poem is too small for everything you are.
But it's yours—like all the pieces of me you helped put together.

She once wore heels and carried files,
A name plate shining on her desk.
Deadlines danced across her days,
And she moved through meetings with quiet grace.

But then, one tiny cry rewrote her plans—
A heartbeat wrapped in smaller hands.
She folded up her dreams like clothes
And placed them in the drawer below.

No resignation letter made the news,
No applause for the path she chose.
Only lullabies, late nights,
And love that never asked for praise.

She traded boardrooms for bedtime stories,
Calendars for lullabies and scraped knees.
Her ambition never died—
It just grew roots in someone else.

Now, the girl who once held her finger
Stands tall with a dream of her own.
And the woman who gave it all up
Smiles quietly from the crowd,
Heart full,
Eyes wet,
Proud beyond words.

Because in every step her daughter takes,
She sees the life she chose—
And wouldn't trade for anything.

2. When His Eyes Spoke First

I held the certificate with shaking hands,
my name printed in gold,
but all I could see—
It was him, my Father.

My father, standing still in the crowd,
Eyes glassy,heart louder than any applause.
He didn't say a word—
he didn't have to.

His tears told every story
We'd lived through together.
The early mornings,
the silent savings,
the dreams he folded into mine.

The times he said,"It's okay, I'll manage,"
Just so I could reach further.
This was not just my victory—
It was his quiet triumph, too.

For every sacrifice he never mentioned,
For every hope he hid behind a calm voice,
For every proud silence he carried
Like a badge.

And in that moment,
I didn't feel like a girl who topped her college—
I felt like a daughter who made her father's dreams
Breathe a little louder.

Yes- He was proud..!!

3. An Empty Plate

Last one for Shambhavi..

The dinner table is full—
of voices, of plates,
of stories passed like salt.

But my eyes still search
for the seat you once filled
without needing to be asked.

You were always late,
but always arrived—laughing, barefoot,
stealing food off my plate
like it was your birthright.

You had no manners,but all the love.
Your fork was a storyteller,
your napkin a witness
to secrets spilled with every bite.

Now there's one less plate,
but your place still lives here.
In the quiet pause before I pass the rice,
in the space beside me
where your elbow used to nudge mine.

No one takes second helpings like you did.
No one tells the stories the same.
And I still pour water
for someone who isn't coming.

Some friendships don't end—they echo.
In the clatter of spoons,
in the laughter that falters,
in every dinnerwhere
I forget for a second that you're not walking through the door.

I miss you most where the food is warm,
and your absencefeels the loudest.

I miss you Shambhavi...!!

4. Evening Chaa

Every evening, like clockwork- Ticking five,
The kettle hums a familiar tune,
Steam rises like memories,
Curling into the corners of home.

She sits by the window,
Old nighty soft with time,
She brings the cups —
one for her, one for him,
More sugar for Maa ,just enough for Baba.

They sip in silence,
but their silence says everything.
A thousand conversations
Steeped into the tea leaves.

Sometimes, he talks about the news,
she nods, half-listening,
stirring her thoughts along with the spoon.
Sometimes, they say nothing at all —
just look out at the sky,side by side or the photo fames on the wall.

The tea cools.
The sun sinks.

But they stay,
as they always have.

Two hands wrapped around warm cups,
Two hearts that have grown old
but never tired of this
Quiet togetherness.

Evening tea —
their pause,
their peace,
their daily love story
Told without a single word.

5. I am Sorry

I am Sorry for being so emotional,
I am Sorry for being so possessive,
I am Sorry that I cry for you,
I am Sorry because I can't live without you..

I am Sorry for the tears you shed,
I am Sorry for the damage I made,
I am Sorry I have made you sick,
Sorry for hurting you so deep..

I am Sorry for giving you sleepless nights,
I am Sorry for each and every fights,
I am Sorry for your pain and agony,
I am Sorry for the missing harmony..

I am Sorry for my Selfish Love,
I am Sorry for not caring enough,
I am Sorry for my restlessness,
I am Sorry for the losing grace..

I am Sorry my friend I made you mad,
I am Sorry darling you are so sad,
Sorry for not giving you any happiness,
Sorry because it's my disgrace..

I am Sorry for thinking of you so much,
I am Sorry I always miss your touch,
I am Sorry of being so made about you,
I am Sorry for my everyday Blue..

I am Sorry of being so immature,
I am Sorry now that can't be cured,
I am Sorry of being myself,
I am Sorry that I've failed..

I am Sorry and Sorry Again,
I am Sorry of being insane,
But believe me, that it was my Love for you
Yes- I Love you
Should I say SORRY for that too??

6. Still watching the door

Oceans apart day after day
And I slowly go insame,
I hear your voice on the line
But it doesn't stop the pain..

If I see you next to never,
How can we stay forever..

Wherever you go,
Whatever you do,
I will be right here waiting for you...
Whatever it takes,
How many heart it breaks,
I will be right here waiting for you...

I took you for granted all the time
Thought it would last somehow,
I hear the laughter, I taste the tears
But I can't get near to you now..

Oh, Can't you see it dear,
You've got me so near.

Wherever you go,
Whatever you do,
I will be right here waiting for you...

Whatever it takes,
How many heart it breaks,
I will be right here waiting for you...

I wonder how will we survive-
Oh, this Romance,
But in the end if I am with you
I'll surely take the chance..

Wherever you go,
Whatever you do,
I will be right here waiting for you...

Whatever it takes,
How many heart it breaks,
I will be right here waiting for you...

I will be waiting for you,
I will be waiting for you watching the door!!

7. If Tomorrow never comes

Sometimes late at night,
I lay awake and watch him sleeping.
He is lost in peaceful dreams,
So I trun out the lights and lay there in the dark.
Thoughts crosses my mind,
What if I never wake up in the morning,
Would he ever doubt the way I feel?
Would he know how my heart longs for him?

If tomorrow never comes,
Will he know how much I love him?
Did I try to show him everyday?
If my time on earth were through,
And he must face the world alone,
Did my love made him strong to stand upright?
Can he answer everyone who was I to him?
If tomorrow never comes!!

'Cause I've lost them all I loved,
Who never wanted to know what's love,
Now they live in regrets - understanding what they lost.
I made a promise, I will tell you everyday

How much I love you night and day..
No second chances are allowed,
What if..
If tomorrow never comes!!

8. Painted a Lie

I want to clear you something,
I don't miss you now
I don't remember the old day
I don't cry when it rainsow
I don't love you anymore..
I know you won't believe this because I am painting a lie...!!

I want to make straight promises to you,
I will never come back to you
I will never shed tears for you
I will always smile in adverse
I will throw away the letters you wrote
I know you won't believe this because I am painting a lie...!!

I want to make sure yoy forget me,
I will try not to appear,
I will not make you happy or sad,
I shall always hurt you as I can,
I would not help you when you need me,
I know you won't believe this because I am painting a lie...!!

I want your heart to hate me,
I don't feel the same way about you,
I lost trust on you,
I wasted my emotions on you,
I stopped breathing your love,
I know you won't believe this because I am painting a lie...!!

Now my eyes are wet, and my lips are dumb—Grief speaks louder than any tongue.
I can not say any more lie
You are my life and Yes I Love You.

I can't think of living apart,
You are the one who freshens up my heart.
You are my morning, my sun through the haze,
You're my last thought at the end of each day.

With you, silence feels like a song,
And time, even heavy, moves along.
You're in my coffee, in evening skies,
In quiet moments and soft goodbyes.

I don't know where I end, or you start—
You live in every beat of my heart.
Believe me or not—this time, it's not a canvas of fiction.

Thank you for enduring my madness,
Thank you for loving me till the end,
Thank you for not believing my lies,
Thank you for everything you are to me..

9. Can anybody find Him

Somebody slowly had taken my heart away,
Somebody slowly had stolen my nights and day,
Somebody cutely smiles when I am alone,
Can anybody find **HIM**?

Somebody had touched me in a lonely place,
Somebody has loved the way I am,
Somebody had only looked deep in my eyes,
Can anybody find **HIM**?

Somebody misses me the whole day,
Somebody carried my name in his heart, but never spoke it aloud,
Somebody tried hard to hide his love from me,
Can anybody find **HIM**?

Somebody had ever looked when I was sad,
Somebody loves me and makes me mad,
Somebody has stopped my flowing tears,
Can anybody find **HIM**?

Somebody holds my hand so tight,
Somebody pull me close to end the fight,
Somebody tied himself through his eyes,
Can anybody find **HIM**?

Somebody has changed my seasons so quick,
Somebody now greets me with shy smiles,
Somebody had made the violen to sing,
Can anybody find **HIM**?

Somebody made the roses more red,
Somebody made the skies go blue,
Somebody had made me say, "I love you",
Can anybody find **HIM**?

Somebody had made salty feel sweet,
Somebody made the toughest subjects feel effortless,
Somebody smiles to make me happy,
Can anybody find **HIM**?

Somebody is my cuddly comfort, always ready to play and stay,
Somebody always tried to be my boy,
Somebody tries to express but feels shy,
Can anybody find **HIM**?

Somebody hides himself to the world,
Someone speaks as if we're strangers in front of people,
Somebody took the pain whenever I fell,
Can anybody find **HIM**?

I bet on it you won't and you can't,
It's just me who knows him well,
And I am all alone who loves him crazy,
Putting my best step forward to cease him for life...

Yet again, Can anybody find **HIM**?

10. Lost

She walks the halls she's always known,
Barefoot on floors she's outgrown.
Walls still whisper her childhood name,
But nothing here feels quite the same.

Her room's the same shade, books still there,
But silence hums in the heavy air.
Her voice once danced in dinner talk,
Now disappears in every walk.

In school she sat in middle rows,
Wrote poems no one ever chose.
Teachers passed with distant eyes,
Marking scores, not silent cries.

In college crowds, she moves unseen,
A ghost between the in-between.
They speak of dreams and bright careers—
She hides behind her laughing peers.

Her mother calls, but doesn't hear
The trembling breath behind "I'm here."
Her father nods, then turns away,
As if love's due on another day.

She's not a stranger, not unknown,
Yet never truly felt at home.
Surrounded, yet she drifts apart—
A lost address inside her heart.

Not lost in woods, nor distant lands,
But in the touch of reaching hands.
She's right there, but no one's guessed—
That being known was her one quest.

So if you pass her in the crowd,
Don't praise the quiet, call it proud.
Some souls get lost, not far, but deep,
In places where they should belong—and weep.

She was **LOST**in all the known places....But she will be found soon!!

11. The Space Between Us

He comes like dusk on a tired day,
Soft-footed, gentle, in shades of gray.
His smile still finds me in a crowd,
But his hand won't stay—it's not allowed.

I watch him leave with eyes that know,
That love like ours must never show.
A wife at home, a child in bed,
A life he chose, where I can't tread.

He tells me things he dares not say
To the ones who see him every day.
He laughs with me, but hides his tears—
We speak in silence, stitched with years.

The boy he lifts upon his back,
The home that waits down every track—
They're not mine, they never were,
Though I once dreamed he'd choose her less sure.

But truth, it settles like evening rain,
So slow, so soft, it whispers pain.
He's fading, not in love—but time—
I am the pause, not the rhyme.

And still he says, "**You were my light, my Sunshine**"
But lights don't warm the loneliest night.
I nod, I smile, I let him be—
While breaking in a way none see.

One day he'll go and never turn,
And I'll remain with what I've learned:
That love can live yet not be free,
And some hearts ache eternally..

12. The Return of Her Light

She was lost, yes—
In rooms with her name on the door,
In voices that never heard hers,
In mirrors that asked "Who are you for?"

But silence taught her how to hear
The pulse beneath her quiet fear.
She built her strength from threadbare days,
And stitched herself in fiercer ways.

No fireworks, no grand parade,
Just steady steps through nights she stayed.
She shaped her pain into resolve,
And turned the world she knew—evolved.

Now halls she walked unseen before
Hold echoes of her growing roar.
The same walls that once closed her in
Now frame the fire born within.

She didn't fight for eyes to see—
She learned the grace of being free.
Success, for her, was not a crown—
It was choosing not to drown.

She smiles now—not to please the crowd,
But because she made herself proud.
And those who once just passed her by
Now stop to ask the reasons why.

But she just nods, and walks ahead—
Alive in ways they never said.
Once lost in all the places known,
She found herself—and stood alone.

That was the return of her light....

13. Yes, More Than a Sister

Yes You weren't born of my blood,
But you were written in my soul.
Not a sister by name or law,
But the one who made me whole.

We built our world in whispers,
Shared secrets no one knew,
You laughed like you belonged to me,
And I believed it too.

I stood beside you, every fall,
And held your trembling hand,
When life got cruel, we stood as one—
An unspoken, sacred band.

But weddings come with silence,
That no vows ever explain,
You wore your gold and vanished,
And left me with the rain.

Now your name feels like a bruise,
On memories that still burn,
I watched you walk into a life
Where I had no return.

You don't call, don't write, don't ask,
As if I was a phase—
As if my love was just a lamp
You lit for darker days.

Betrayal doesn't always shout—
Sometimes it softly stays,
In dinners missed, in words unsent,
In all the empty grays.

And still, I do not curse your name,
I just mourn who you became.
Because love like mine was never fake—
But you forgot, and that's the ache.

Yes, you were more than a Sister,
Alas! that's the truth..

14. Not a Doctor, But Still Me

I once held dreams in tiny palms,
Of stethoscopes and healing balms.
A white coat hung in every prayer,
A future drawn with tender care.

I saw myself in hospital halls,
Saving lives within sterile walls.
My heart beat with a healer's fire—
But life rerouted that desire.

Doors I knocked on stayed shut tight,
Paths I chased slipped out of sight.
The dream I cradled since a child,
Faded slow, but left me wild.

So I turned to books, to questions deep,
To truths the world had yet to keep.
And word by word, and thought by thought,
I stitched a life the stars had brought.

A PhD—not what I planned,
But built with my own calloused hands.
No scalpels here, no patients' cries,
But still, I chase the "how" and "why."

And now I stand with open grace,
Not in white, but in my place.
I may not heal with tools or charts,
But I still serve with mind and heart.

So if you ask me who I am—
Not the dream, but all I became—
I'll smile and say, "I took the fall,
But still I rose—and that is all."

15. The Tiffin Box

It started with a tiny hand,
And a bag too big to hold,
A school bell rang, a morning rush,
And a tiffin wrapped in foil.

Parathas cut in perfect shapes,
Sometimes a note inside—
"Eat well, my moon, be kind, be brave,"
With all her love supplied.

In school, I'd trade a bite or two,
But never gave it whole—
For every bite held warmth from home,
A piece of her gentle soul.

Then came college, hostel days,
But she'd still pack with care,
Stuffing boxes on the train,
With "I know you'll miss it there."

And now I walk in office shoes,
Deadlines stacked and days that blur,
But every noon, I pause awhile—
To open a box that smells like her.

Rice and sabzi, rolls or stew,
Sometimes the same old treat—
But nothing tastes like her handmade love,
That turns a meal complete.

She never missed a single day,
In sunshine or in rain,
Through exams, mistakes, and job fatigue,
Her love has stayed the same.

Not all heroes wear a cape,
Some wear a cotton sari or Salwar suits like mine,
And fight the world with spices stirred
At five each morning, softly.

So if you see me smile at lunch,
Know it's not just food, you see—
It's every year she stood behind,
Still feeding strength to me.

16. अनकही

Unspoken words

कुछ बातें छुपी-छुपाई सीआँखों में देखी जाती हैं,
\लब खामोश हैं फिर भीकहानियाँ कही जाती हैं।

हर रोज़ मुलाक़ातों मेंकुछ वक़्त चुप रहता है,
पर दिल की धड़कनों सेइक राज़ सा बहता है।

न कोई वादा, न इज़हार,फिर भी सब कुछ होता है,
ये जो रिश्ता है बेआवाज़बहुत कुछ कह जाता है।

मुस्कुरा दे वो जो एक बार,हँस के हम दिल हार जाएँगे।
फिर भी दिल डरता है,क्या हम उसको पाएँगे?

वो ख्वाबों में हर रात मिले,पर हक़ीक़त में खो जाती है,
हर बार दिल कहता है कुछ,और ज़ुबाँ चुप रह जाती है।

उसकी चुप्पी में भी बात है,उसकी नज़रों में भी राज़ है,
हम तो बस उसे देख केख़ुद से भी बेग़ाने हो जाते हैं।

क़दम रुकते हैं सोचकर,कहीं वो दूर न हो जाए,
कहीं हम जो चाहें उसे,वो हमें अपना न बनाए।

थम सी जाती हैं ये साँसें,तुम सामने जब बैठे रहते हो।
प्यार अगर है तुम्हें भी,तो तुम दुनिया से क्यों डरते हो?

साथ जो दो तुम मेरा अभी,हम सारी उम्र निभाएँगे।
वादा अभी ये मैंने किया,कभी न दूर जाएँगे।

हम देंगे उधार तुम्हें हँसी,अगर तुम ग़म में खो जाओ तो,
हम बनेंगे साया तुम्हारा,अगर तुम अकेले रह जाओ तो।

हम देंगे हाथ तुम्हें अगर,तुम राह में गिर जाओ तो,
हम देंगे साथ तुम्हारा,अगर तुम टूट के बिखर जाओ तो।

मंज़िलें मुश्किल हो सकती हैं,पर सफ़र आसान हो जाएगा,
अगर तुम्हारा हाथ थाम लें,तो हर ज़ख्म भी मुस्कान हो जाएगा।

बस इतना फिर से कहना है,हमें इंतज़ार उस दिन का रहेगा,
जब दोनों के दिल मिलेंगे,और प्यार ही प्यार बहेगा।

इतना सब कुछ कहना था, कितना सब कुछ सुनना था,

रहे गई वो बाते **"अनकही"**, जो कहानी तुम से बुनना था.॥

17. थोड़े तुम, थोड़े हम

A little you, a little me —Together we became a complete world.

थोड़े तुम, थोड़े हम,
मिल जाएँ तो बन जाए जीवन का संगम।

तुम्हारी ख़ामोशी में भी कुछ बातें हैं,
मेरी उलझनों में भी सौ राहतें छुपी हैं।
तुम आधा कह के रुक जाते हो,
मैं अधूरी बातों को पूरी समझ लेती हूँ।

थोड़े तुम, थोड़े हम,
हर झगड़े के बाद भी एक हैं हम।

तुम्हारी आदतें मुझे खलती भी हैं,
पर उन्हीं में अपनापन भी दिखता है।
मैं कभी ज़िद कर लेती हूँ बेवजह,
और तुम मुस्कुरा कर हार मान जाते हो।

थोड़े तुम, थोड़े हम,
मिल कर बन जाएँ एक मुकम्मल ग़ज़ल हम।

तुम चाँद जैसे, मैं रात सी,
तुम हवा जैसे, मैं बात सी।
तुम्हारे बिना अधूरा हूँ मैं,
और मेरी बिना तुम भी ख़ामोश से।

थोड़े तुम, थोड़े हम,
इस रिश्ते के दोनों ही अहम।

ना तुम पूरे, ना मैं पूरी,
फिर भी साथ में एक पूरी दुनिया सी।
प्यार यूँ ही नहीं होता बेवजह,
इसमें थोड़ा तुम, थोड़ा मैं हर दफा।

18. बस इतना कहना था

(Bas itna kehna tha —I just wanted to say —to ones who judged my skintone)

कभी मेरे रंग पर हँसते थे,
जैसे सावला होना,
कोई गुनाह हो।
तुम्हारी नज़र में मैं,
"दोस्ती के लायक" ही नहीं थी।

तुम्हारी टोली में जगह न सही,
पर मेरी मेहनत में हिम्मत थी।
तुम ठहरे रंग-परखने वाले,
मैं ठहर गई सपनों की भूखी।

आज मैं वहाँ खड़ी हूँ,
जहाँ पहुँचने की सोच से भी,
तुम्हारे पाँव काँपते हैं।
मेरी ऊँचाई से तुम्हारी हँसी,
अब बहुत छोटी लगती है।

याद रखना—रंग सिर्फ़ त्वचा का होता है,
औक़ात मेहनत से बनती है।
और हाँ...बस इतना कहना था,

अब मेरी छाया में खड़े होकर,
धूप की बातें मत करना।

तुम्हारे लिए मैं बस एक चेहरा थी,
जिसे न अपनाना ही बेहतर था,
तुम्हारे क़दम मेरे साथ नहीं,
पर तुम्हारी हँसी, मेरे पीछे चलती थी।

आज वही क़दम मैं अकेले बढ़ा चुकी हूँ,
उन राहों पर जहाँ तुम्हारी नज़र भी नहीं पहुँचती,
मेरी मेहनत का रंग
तुम्हारे सोच से कहीं गहरा है।

अब जब मेरी पहचान,
मेरे रंग से नहीं,
मेरे काम से होती है,
बस इतना कहना था—
धूप से डरने वालों,
सूरज बनकर जीना, और बात है।

19. एक तुम्हारा, एक मेरा हिस्सा

(एक लड़की की कलम से – अपने दूर बैठे प्रेमी के लिए)

कहते हैं प्यार पास होने से नहीं चलता,
पर दूर रहकर हर पल तुम्हें महसूस करना...
वो आसान भी नहीं होता।

एक तुम्हारा, एक मेरा हिस्सा —
बँट चुका है दिल यूँ, जैसे बिन कहे कोई वादा हो।

तुम वहाँ हो, मैं यहाँ,
पर फिर भी हर धड़कन में तुम हो,
और हर साँस में मैं।

तुम्हारी हँसी की गूँज अब भी कानों में है,
जैसे वो आख़िरी मुलाक़ात अभी-अभी गुज़री हो।
मैं अब भी उसी मोड़ पर हूँ,
जहाँ तुमने कहा था — "जल्दी मिलेंगे।"

कभी लगता है, आधी हूँ मैं...
वो आधा हिस्सा तुम अपने साथ ले गए।
अब जो भी सोचती हूँ, उसमें "हम" होता है,
"मैं" कहीं पीछे छूट गई हूँ।

दिन के शोर में भी एक सन्नाटा होता है,
शाम की चाय फीकी सी लगती है।
हर बात जो अधूरी रह जाती है,
वो रात के तकिये में छिपकर रोती है।

पर जानती हूँ,तुम भी वहीं कहीं बैठे हो,
मेरी ही तरह — अधूरे, पर वफ़ादार।
तुम्हारे हिस्से का प्यारहर रोज़ मेरे नाम
एक खामोश ख़त बनकर आता है।

मैं सोचती हूँ, जब मिलेंगे फिर से,
तो क्या हम पहचान पाएँगे एक-दूजे को?
या हमारी ख़ामोशियाँ ही बोलेंगी —
वो सब जो लफ़्ज़ कह नहीं पाए।

तुम्हारा हिस्सा — मेरा इंतज़ार है।
मेरा हिस्सा — तुम्हारी यादों का संसार है।
जब मिलेंगे फिर,तो शायद वक़्त भी रुक जाएगा,
और कहेगा —"अब सब पूरा है।"

एक तुम्हारा, एक मेरा हिस्सा —
मिलकर बनेगा फिर से हमारा जहाँ।
जब तुम पास आओगे,
तो अधूरी मैं — फिर से मुकम्मल बन जाऊँगी।

20. है अगर ख़ुदा, तो वो है कहाँ..

है अगर ख़ुदा, तो वो है कहाँ?
वो सामने क्यों नहीं आते?
मुझे बात करनी है उनसे —

21. Forgotten Flower

Once, I bloomed in the shadow,
where no sunlight dared to stay.
Feet passed,eyes glanced,
but none stopped to know my name.

The garden was full of voices,
bright petals laughed in the open air,
their colors painting the morning,
while I stood quietlyin a corner of cracked earth.

The wind carried whispers of brighter petals,
the rain caressed gardens far away.
I learned the language of patience,
counting seasons in silence,
collecting strength in my roots,
while I stood in the corner,
unnoticed,
unclaimed.

They thought I would wither,
fold in on myself and vanish,
but I had a pact with the soil—
to endure,
to wait for my moment.

One morning, without fanfare,
the clouds broke.
A single ray of sunlight
slid across the earthand found me.

I opened again—not for them,
not for the footsteps that once ignored me,
but for the sky,
for the wind that carried my scent,
for the rain that had never forgotten me.

And now, when they pass,
they stop.
They ask my name.
They wonder how I survived.
But I smile in my silence—
for even a forgotten flower
can teach the world
that beauty does not need witnesses
to grow.

22. Lamborghini

Beneath a quilt of Adriatic blue,
she sleeps, the sea's hush cradling her sigh,
moonlight spilled through lace-curtained windows,
soft as the breath of summer on her cheek.

In dreams, she slips behind the wheel—
a Crimson Lamborghini, purring like midnight thunder,
its mirror-slick body catching the stars
as if they were born only to follow her.

The road winds between whitewashed houses,
their tiled roofs kissed by bougainvillea blooms,
gardens spilling rosemary, figs, and lavender,
the scent rising to greet her through an open window.

Olive groves lean in like curious old friends,
and the cliffs drop away to a turquoise hush,
waves folding over themselves in slow applause
for the girl who rides light in her sleep.

She does not wake.
The engine hum becomes a heartbeat,
and in that Croatian night—
the car,
the road,

the sea,
are hers forever.

As she wakes up, her eyes are still searching
Her red Chariot,
Sudden realisation of someone else was sitting with her on her Coupe,
Made her smile and close her eyes again...
Trying to find the face.

But morning spills gold through the shutters,
warm on her brow.
She opens her eyes finally—
and the dream is broken with a smile.

23. School Bus

The bus was already a blue-white blur written "A"

at the end of the lane—
its windows glinting like it knew
she was late first time.
She skidded to the stop,
breath sharp,but the driver didn't see,
and the hiss of the engine
was already a goodbye.
Then came the rickshaw—her saviour,
paint peeling, horn singing,
like a sidekick stumbling into the plot.
She leapt in, stood tall on the back—shouted let's GO,
wind slapping her hair into wild banners.
The street blurred,
shops and trees rushing past
as she leaned forward,
hands gripping the frame of the rikshaw seat,
Superhero Cape missing but heart flying,
the city her runway.
And there—the bus,
slowing at the next corner stoppage.
She jumped down,feet hitting the ground like a landing

hero, breathless, grinning,
she was her own morning legend today.

Her first **Morning Chase- her School bus.**

24. The House That Dreamed Me

We came for the weekend,
a quiet holiday in the hills—
an old wooden house,
its bones creaking with the wind,
its walls smelling of rain and secrets.

By day, sunlight crawled through the windows
like a lazy cat.
By night, the silence grew thick,
and the shadows listened.

That first night,
I dreamed of hallways that bent in wrong directions,
doors that opened to endless staircases,
mirrors where my reflection
stood half a second too still.

I saw a girl in those dreams—
pale as moonlight,
her hair wet as if from rain,
her smile…
too wide to belong to any joy I knew.

I ran through the house in the dream,
but every room was the same room,

every corner turned me back
to where I began.

The wind outside
sounded like someone whispering my name,
and somewhere between heartbeats
I felt a cold hand brush my cheek.

Then—a sudden fall,
a gasp,
I woke.
But I did not wake in my bed.

The same house surrounded me—
the same cracked wallpaper,
the same shivering curtains.

Only the world outside the window
was dark as ink.

And there she was.
The girl.

Standing in the garden,
looking straight at me.
Her dress clung to her like water.
Her smile
was the same one from my dream.

She lifted a hand—
not to wave,
but to beckon.

My heart thundered.
I turned to call for my family—
and found them standing in the doorway,
their eyes wide,
astonished,
as if they had just woken from the same dream.

"Don't open the window," my mother whispered,
but her voice cracked—
and I noticed
her hair was wet.

The girl outside tilted her head,
and suddenly I saw…
she wasn't standing on the ground.
Her feet hovered,
just above the grass.

The glass between us grew colder,
my breath fogging it into shapes—
letters—
my name.

I blinked,
and she was gone.
But when I turned back,
the window was open,
and the curtains swayed
as if someone had just stepped inside.

I froze,every nerve strung tight.
The air behind me was still—
too still.

Then, from the garden,
through the night air thick as syrup,
I heard a voice.
My voice.

Calling softly,urgently—
"Come out… it's safe now."

I turned back to the window.
The girl was there again,
but now…
she wore my face.

And she smiled.

25. Veil

They say she came from the edge of a map
where ink fades into whispers.
No one remembers her arriving,
only that the air felt different after.

She walks as if the earth rearranges itself
just to keep her path hidden.
Each step writes a sentence in dust—
and the wind edits it before you can read.

Some claim her voice tastes like autumn,
all smoke and orchard-sweetness,
but others swear they've only heard silence,
and that was enough to haunt them.

Her smile is a door
that leads to a room with no floor.
You either fall forever,
or find wings you didn't know you had.

Her hands hold stories
that no pen has dared to write,
and her eyes—
two locked rooms without a key.

Once, I followed her to the pier at dawn.
The water mirrored her perfectly—
but when I looked back,
she was gone,and the reflection kept moving.

Maybe she is a memory
from someone else's life,
slipped into mine by mistake.
Maybe she's a ghost waiting for a story.

Or maybe she is just a woman—
but one who knows how to vanish
without ever leaving.

26. Birthdays Across the Map

Each year the calendar turns a page,
and the candles flicker, marking my age.
But for me, a birthday's more than a day—
it's a journey, a memory, a magical getaway.

From the very first breath that I took in this world,
Mom and Dad were the sails in my ship, unfurled.
Without them, I'd have no skies to roam,
no seas to sail, no place called home.

One year it was **Pondicherry's**golden shore,
French streets and sunsets I still adore.
We sipped on the breeze, walked by the tide,
with laughter and love as our only guide.

Then **Malaysia**called with a tropical hue,
Petronas city lights, islands, and skies so blue.
Markets alive with colors and song,
holding their hands, I felt I belonged.

The **Andaman**waves whispered to me,
secrets of corals beneath the sea.
Every splash was a gift, each dive a thrill,
but my parents' smiles were the magic still.

In **Kodaikanal's**misty embrace,
we found a quiet, gentle place.
Lakes and hills wrapped us around,
in every leaf, their love I found.

Ooty'stea-scented mountain air
made every birthday moment rare.
Toy trains, gardens, skies so wide—
but the joy was walking by their side.

Through **Gujarat's**desert, rich and old,
we wandered where stories and legends are told.
White sands in the Rann, under moonlight's gleam,
a birthday felt like a living dream.

Kashmir—oh, heaven's own land,
with snowy peaks and rivers so grand.
Shikara rides and saffron fields,
and warmth only my family yields.

In **Udupi**, temples by the sea,
blessings fell like waves on me.
And Malpe's golden, endless beach
taught me joy is in what love can reach.

And **Darjeeling**, where the mountains wake,
and tea gardens paint each rolling lake.
The toy train sang, the clouds would play,
marking another beautiful birthday day.

Each trip a chapter, each year a song,
yet the heart of it all has been there all along—

Mom and Dad, my compass and chart,
the anchor, the sails, the beating heart.

No matter how far my journeys will run,
I'll always be your little one.
For every candle, every cheer,
I owe the reason I'm here.

And as the years keep turning, you'll see—
no matter the place, I'll always be me.
Your daughter, your joy, your unchanging light,
loving you both with all my might.

27. Leaving the Nest for Good

I thought the nest was shelter,
a place of arms and light,
but feathers hid the splinters
and warmth was never right.

They said, "We are your family,"
but family should not fade
when storms press hard against you,
when skies are cold and grey.

It's you who holds yourself up,
and those who choose to stay—
the ones who fight beside you,
not just when skies are gay.

Blood is not the measure,
nor names upon a tree.
It's love that shows in actions,
it's trust that sets you free.

So I spread my wings unshaken,
and fly where hearts are true,
leaving the nest for good this time—
for my real "**home**" is you.

My family is where my **MOM and DAD**lives.

28. Animal Planet

Somewhere beyond the blue of the skies,
lies a land with a thousand eyes—
not from stars, but from creatures bright,
watching the day, guarding the night.

Lions yawn in golden heat,
paws heavy on the earth's heartbeat.

Penguins waddle in tuxedo pride,
while dolphins dance with the silver tide.

Parrots paint the air with sound,
Elephants shake the shaking ground.

Foxes write secrets in the snow,
and Fireflies make the moonlight glow.

Turtles sail through coral seas,
Whales hum ballads to the breeze.

Monkeys swing where rivers run,
and Zebras graze in stripes of sun.

Butterflies stitch the morning air,
Pandas dream without a care.

Owls keep watch with moonlit eyes,
as Bats draw maps across the skies.

Here, no voice is lost or small,
every roar and chirp belongs to all.
The wind carries every tale and song—
a wild, bright world where we all belong.

For Animal Planet is not just a show,
it's the home of life in its brightest glow—
a reminder, each heartbeat, fur, and feather,
that we and the wild are bound together.

29. Teddy on the Swing

I sit upon the wooden seat,
the ropes creak softly, slow, and sweet.
The breeze rocks me from side to side,
yet all I feel is the empty tide.

Once, your hands would hold me tight,
we'd soar together in golden light.
Your laughter spilled like summer rain,
and I, your teddy, forgot all pain.

The swing would fly, the sky would sing,
and I was more than a stitched-up thing.
A pilot, a knight, a brave balloon—
we touched the clouds, we kissed the moon.

But days have passed, and seasons turned,
the garden quiet, the candles burned.
Your footsteps echo here no more,
no shadow dances by the door.

I watch the sparrows come and go,
I feel the sun, I taste the snow.
The roses bloom, the evenings fall,
but none of it matters without your call.

I miss the way you brushed my fur,
the silly songs, the whispered blur
of dreams you shared when no one knew—
those secrets live, still stitched, still true.

Sometimes the swing moves on its own,
as if the wind recalls what's gone.
And I pretend it's you again,
pushing me higher through joy and rain.

I am only cotton, button, thread,
but I hold the life that we both led.
And though the world has pulled you away,
I sit and wait for another day.

For love does not fade, though time may roam,
this swing, this garden, will be our home.
And I—your teddy, worn but true—
will always be waiting here for you.

30. We will meet again..!!

In this lifetime, love, the roads are long,
twisting turns where we don't belong.

The world has built its walls so high,
yet still, I whisper your name to the sky.

I hold you close in a hidden place,
a shadowed dream, a fleeting trace.

Though miles and years may stretch between,
my heart remembers where you have been.

We walk apart, yet breathe the same air,
a secret tether, unseen but there.

And though this life may keep us away,
another dawn waits, another day.

Perhaps in a world the stars design,
your hand in mine will fully align.

No chains of fate, no heavy pain—
only the promise: we will meet again.

So if you feel lonely, broken, or far,
look to the night and find my star.

For love like ours cannot decay,
it waits for us—beyond today.